WAITING FOR OUR FOREVER HOME

Written by: Marie Annette Chorovich

Co-Authored by: Barbara L. Goodin

Illustrated by: Mia Maecher

Dedicated by Marie to Justen, Kassi, Kendall, Calil,
Tenzin, Tristen, Rogers, Rainbow and my sister Kathy
who always believed in me.

Sunday, June 21st, 2020 at 2:00 PM turned out to be a very TERRIFIC day. It would be a life-changing experience for my brother Stuart and me. It was a sunny 85 degrees and officially the first full day of summer. Stuart and I were living in the Berea Animal Shelter, which is located 16 miles south of Cleveland, Ohio.

My name is Bob. I am a very orange and white kitten, while Stuart has a lot of black, gray, and white fur and a very fluffy tail. You would never guess that we are brothers.

Every Monday for about three months, someone named Marie called the shelter looking for a very orange kitten to adopt. Pat would always seem to answer the phone and tell Marie that they had a very orange kitten named Bob, but he was not old enough to be adopted. She also told Marie that Bob had a brother named Stuart in case she wanted two kittens. My brother and I lived in a huge silver cage. It was a nice place for two kittens to live, but it didn't feel like a forever home.

After six more weeks, we finally heard Pat say
the very orange kitten and his brother were ready to
be adopted. Stuart and I looked at each other and
hoped she was talking about us. When Pat got off the
phone, she told us Marie would be coming to take us
home today. We jumped for joy and gave each other
a high five.

Stuart and I started to watch the clock. Time was moving very slowly. At 10:00 no one showed up. At 11:00 no one yet. At noon, we decided to take a nap. At 2:00 a lady walked in and said,"My name is Marie and I'm here to adopt a very orange kitten and a black, gray, and white kitten with a very fluffy tail."

One of the volunteers was asked to show the orange kitten to Marie. As I was leaving the cage, I told Stuart I hoped he would be joining me. When they handed me to Marie, she held me so tightly and kissed me on my little cute nose and I started to purr. Marie was wearing aviator sunglasses, pants with a pattern of cats, a cat shirt, cat tennis shoes, a yellow purse with cats on it, and a kitten watch.

I was thrilled to know Marie must be a real cat lover.

Tracy, from the animal shelter, explained all of the information about kittens and gave Marie many forms to fill out.

Marie told the volunteer she wanted to adopt me, and she also wanted to meet my brother Stuart. When they put Stuart in Marie's arms, she held him so tightly and kissed him on his little cute nose, and he started to purr. Stuart and I were so happy to hear that Marie wanted to adopt both of us.

The volunteers waved goodbye to both of us and said, "We love you, Bob and Stuart!" Marie told them that Bob will be named Summer, and Stuart will be named Star. She said Star and I should think of her as Mom instead of Marie. Marie put Star and me in our brand new cat carrier.

When Mom got to the car, she made sure our cat carrier was buckled in. Mom told us we would be living in North Royalton, Ohio, which is 19 miles south of Cleveland. She told us we would have a lot of toys.

Mom was right! The apartment looked like an amusement park with three large cat trees, a tent that looked like a circus tent, another tent with a gigantic tunnel to play in, toys that lit up, toys that made funny sounds, and a couch made of fur to nap on. Also, on the second floor, there was a huge balcony.

We were on the second floor and so high up. Mom said we would spend many days on the balcony watching the birds and butterflies and watching the flowers grow. I looked at Star and said,"We really hit the jackpot! This apartment is amazing!" We could tell that Mom had spent a lot of time cleaning and designing such a beautiful apartment. When we went in her bedroom, we were told that Mom hoped both of us would sleep with her every night.

Today, Mom told us about three REALLY good friends! Mom wanted us to meet them before the kitten shower. First, we met her sister Kathy, then Barb, and then we met Audrey. Mom had known Barb for 65 years and Audrey for 48 years! The three of them do fun stuff together. Kathy, Barb, and Audrey said we were just SO cute! When Mom heard that, she smiled a lot.

    After we were settled in our forever home, Mom explained to us that there were some rules that were very important. She said, "First of all, you both have to share all of your toys. Also, you have so many toys that there is no reason to fight over them. When our friends come over, we'll let them pick first what toy they would like to play with."

Mom continued, "Lastly, we are not allowed to BULLY anyone. EVER! We must never make fun of any of the animals in the world."

A week after we arrived, Mom threw a kitten shower to introduce us to her friends. We made our grand entrance in a beautiful pink stroller. All of her friends were so excited to see and meet us for the first time. The guests donated money to the Berea Animal Shelter, and Mom's friends bought many more gifts for us.

Star and I found out that Mom had a friend named Mary Ann, and she had invited us for a play date to meet her new kitten Tipper. We could already imagine all three of us splashing around in Tipper's swimming pool.

We are Summer and Star and we are no longer waiting for our forever home because we have found it with our new mom. She tells us that we would have many more fun adventures!

THE END

...or is it only the beginning?

Summer

Star

Rainbow

Rogers

Illustrator- Mia Maechner

Author- Marie Chorovich   Co-author-Barbara Goodin

Please note:

Sprinkled throughout this book are different colors of the same cat drawn by a little boy on the Autism Spectrum. While there is no cure, early detection and intensive early treatment can make a significant difference in the lives of many of these children.